My Poetry Idol

Inspirations

Edited By Sarah Washer

First published in Great Britain in 2017 by:

Coltsfoot Drive
Peterborough
PE2 9BF
Telephone: 01733 890066
Website: www.youngwriters.co.uk

All Rights Reserved
Book Design by Jenni Harrison
© Copyright Contributors 2017
SB ISBN 978-1-78624-926-5
Printed and bound in the UK by BookPrintingUK
Website: www.bookprintinguk.com
YB0304W

Foreword

Dear Reader,

Our latest competition, *My Poetry Idol,* focuses on the people that these young poets look up to. Using a mix of imagination, expression and poetic styles, this anthology is an impressive snapshot of the inventive, original and skilful writing of young people today, expressing their appreciation for the people, and things, that mean the most to them.

Young Writers was established in 1991 to nurture creativity in our children and young adults, to give them an interest in poetry and an outlet to express themselves. Seeing their work in print will encourage them to keep writing as they grow and become our poets of tomorrow.

Selecting the poems has been challenging and immensely rewarding. The effort and imagination invested by these young writers makes their poems a pleasure to enjoy reading time and time again. It also made picking a winner a very difficult task, so well done to Laura Farrell who has won a selection of books and a hamper for her moving poem.

Sarah Washer

Contents

Winner:

Laura Farrell (17)   1

Independent Entries

Umaymah Abrar (13)	3
Abigail Ann Bywater (16)	4
Sayon Choudhuri (12)	6
Adaora Elliott (14)	8
Jodie Stone (13)	10
Nour Tazaoui (14)	12
Nikisha Bhogaita (16)	14
Yasmin Batoul Rafiq (12)	16
Naomi Salumu Ngwewa (10)	17
Cecile Kwarteng (12)	18
Sabrina Priyanka Azmi (15)	19
Urooj Rahimi (9)	20
Lana Masood Ahmed (13)	22
Ella-Rose Mulcare (16)	23
Faizah Hussain (11)	24
Chloe Chuck (14)	25
Zineb Ait Ziane (9)	26
Shannon Rose Byrne (15)	27
Dathusan Thavaneswaran (6)	28
Jessica Nelson (12)	29
Romer Palad (16)	30
Carmel Temilore Oniye (10)	31
Koryn Archer (10)	32
Aaria Bains (6)	33
Rishika Raghunandanan (12)	34
Prince Opara (10)	35
Megan Williams (9)	36
Jocelyn Ngomabie (10)	37
Ashley James (14)	38
Satiya Yaya (14)	39
Maddi Davis (12)	40
Oliver Poole (8)	41
Georgia Anne Ellis (12)	42
Paavun Kaur (9)	43
Katie Muckells (10)	44
Jasmine Lily Bloor (12)	45
Mya Coco-Bassey (14)	46
Rashidah Ajayi (10)	47
Tanica Cherelle Karen Anderson (13)	48
Thaila Smith (12)	49
Sophie Rea (13)	50
Nimrah Jan (7)	51
Samerah Khan Bi (11)	52
Hannah Forster (12)	53
Anya Linda Kozlowski (10)	54
Rimsha Shoukat (17)	55
Shazia Rahman (15)	56
Charley Anders (7)	57
Misty Worofka (13)	58
Tayla Alison Schofield (13)	59
Jack Mascot (9)	60
Sithija Kurukulasuriya (5)	61
Ebubechukwu Chidubem Onwuzurigbo (8)	62
Lina Jabeen (10)	63
Veronika Andersone (11)	64
Connie Power	65

Bamford Academy, Rochdale

Atira Todd (10)	66
Isabelle Baker (10)	67
Daisy Parton (10)	68
Laila Kaysor (10)	69
Amber Aslam (7)	70

Haniya Arien (6)	71
Harry Hoyle (10)	72
Aleeza Azam (7)	73
Charlie James Magnall (7)	74
Esme Coulton	75
Joseph Samuel Thomas (9)	76
Aisha Khawaja (7)	77

King Edward VI Handsworth School For Girls, Birmingham

Hiba Waseem (12)	78
Anika Sowan (12)	80
Jaskeerat Kaur Gill (13)	82
Holly Wiseman (12)	84
Esha Din (12)	86
Nadine Bowie-Fox (12)	88
Sophie Dang (13)	89
Maariya Khan (13)	90
Rebecca Sofia Middleton (13)	92
Madleen Mohammad (12)	94
Mary Hoggard (13)	96
Simran Nandhra (12)	97
Safaa Arooj Taj (12)	98
Harneek Sandhu (12)	99
Visvesa Modi (13)	100
Uzma Amin (13)	102
Jerusha Jeyasuthan (12)	103
Gursimran Kaur (12)	104
Ponal Qureshi (12)	105
Kate Holmes (12)	106
Arfah Khan (12)	107
Chenyao Zhou (12)	108
Gurleen Klair (12)	109
Shriya Kashyap (12)	110
Ayesha Sarfraz (12)	111
Emily Warmington (12)	112
Gurmeena Kaur Nahal (13)	113
Abigail Balfour (12)	114
Nancy Alice Rutter (13)	115
Hana Amin (12)	116
Nizara Ziaudeen (12)	117
Iqra Rehman (12)	118
Isabella Hickman (13)	119
Dhairya Ruparelia (12)	120
Audrey Ntelah (12)	121
Ramisa Mumith (12)	122

Sanquhar Academy, Sanquhar

Rhiannon Flynn (13)	123
Keira Cunningham (12)	124
Kerri Louise Freeburn (14)	125
Hannah Kenyon (13)	126

The Poems

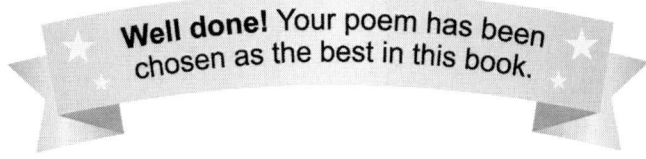

Always

He always sang
My grandpa
Unfamiliar tunes with ridiculous lyrics,
Perfectly timed for imperfect moments,
Followed by 'Top of the Pops, 19xx'.
A family idiom,
It didn't matter that he was always wrong.

He always sang obnoxiously,
The life of dead family gatherings.
Scolded by a long-suffering wife,
And encouraged by us kids who knew no better,
A forced smile from those who'd heard the same song again
And again, always.

It would be 'easy' to get over it
If what was him was dead long before he died
But like a cuckoo clock,
Little glimpses of 'Grandpa' popped through,
Less and less often as time ticked by.

The last time that bird popped out
He sang
'Happy birthday,' to me
In half-formed words and warbling tunes
With all the other poor souls in the home
While I stood there, awkward,
Not knowing that that moment would be the last of 'Grandpa'.

A month after,
Brother's eighteenth.
He wasn't there to sing.
But we were
And we will
For you, Grandpa,
Always.

Laura Farrell (17)

My Angel: My Mother

There is no one like you, Mom
You are just the best
You are a wonderful mother
No matter what decision I take you are with me
All the ways you show you care
Always make me feel I am a part of you
Even within a crowd you are there to support me
As a child I felt you would hold my hand then
And later will let go
But now I know my mom has and will hold my heart forever
You know what, this is no illusion, it's hope, belief in you Mom
You make broken look beautiful and weak look strong
You walk with a universe on your shoulders and make it look like a pair of wings
Mom, I am sorry for all the mistakes I made
You might not be proud of me, I might be a disappointment to you
But I promise I'll try my best to make you a proud mum
I hope you know how sorry I am and how much I love you today
In the past I didn't realise how words can break hearts
Leave scars that last a lifetime and tear two lives apart
I thank you Mom because I didn't know what you sacrificed as I grew
You're my angel
It feels like a dream, yet so true!

Umaymah Abrar (13)

The Lonesome Girl

I'll tell you something about a girl I know,
that being said, this girl also happens to be my best friend...
The problem with this girl is that she constantly seeks conversation.
I am so sick and tired of everyone that she talks to
treating her like a dead rodent at the side of the road.
This girl is spectacular, that opinion may be biased, but let me explain,
she is literally my diamond in the rough
and she doesn't give herself enough credit.
That being said it absolutely destroys me to
see person after person break her heart or let her down,
I'm not joking when I say she is the
most beautiful human I've laid eyes on
and it's such a disappointment to see her being treated
like she isn't important because she is more than important,
she is a diamond.
She is quiet and she is shy at first
but she is so bubbly and energetic once she lets you in,
I find it hard to believe how someone could abuse her kindness and trust.
She was there for me in my darkest times
and somehow always finds the right words to bring me back to life.
Although we may argue she is a literal star
and I will always have her back no matter what the circumstance
because she is not only my best friend
but she's my soul mate in a platonic way.

Seeing her in a bad place drags me down to the bad place
and motivates me to do my best to drag us both out alive.
If she wasn't by my side I'm not sure how I would have been able
to find my way today,
she is like the sun and I am the Earth beneath.
She sheds light on my life and I am forever grateful,
forever smiling but also so very naive.
When she is self-conscious about how she looks
I will be there to remind her that I love the little things she hates
about herself
because when I look at such a beauty, she deserves so much more
than these people she falls for,
she deserves love and appreciation
thus I am here to love the little things
and remind her each and every day that she is worth it
and she is beautiful.
She gives me hope when nothing else does
and although she can be outrageously moody on occasions
she is also the most adorable human I've ever come across
which is why it is so difficult to understand why anyone would
want to mistreat her because she is enough for me and I could sit
here and promote her all day
but I know that I love her and I will do everything in my power
to make sure she is safe and she is loved
whether she wants me to or not because she is worth it,
in darkness she is all I see and all I need
and I hope she is by my side for a very long time because she is
my angel.

Abigail Ann Bywater (16)

My Idol

He will be forever in my heart
Forever and ever he has done his part,
To make me who I am now.
Never too much sweat upon his brow.

Yes, I can tell you are bursting to know.
But for that you'll have to wait till the end of the show
His qualities don't come with any fee
He has always been there beside me.

He isn't anyone off the street
As he cares for me from his hair to his feet
I have always looked up to him and will do so evermore.
He has taught me everything he knows and even more.

Whenever I am in need, I have somewhere to go
He has always been my friend and never my foe
He is the one to tell all my thoughts and feelings
For I know he won't discard them as orange peelings

As to who my idol is, I won't be keeping you bereft
So much to say about him but there's not much left.
I'd better continue swiftly on
For I'd like this to be over before dawn

My idol is kind but firm
Which is necessary for a child to learn
To all my idol says, I listen
After which, within my brain, the orb of knowledge glistens

My idol may not have been a celebrity
But he is great for his humanity
Without him, I don't know whether I would have been such a fine lad
For yes, you are my idol and I love you, Dad.

Sayon Choudhuri (12)

Parasocial Relationships

Parasocial relationships are a kind of relationship between you and someone you don't actually know.
An actor, a musician, a YouTuber, a character in a book.
Some people may say it's stupid.
Some people may say it is dumb.
Some people may say I don't know them,
But all that matters is that I feel I do.

I *know* that they're good people.
Whether they're real or fake or famous.
I know that they'll do the right thing when it's hard
and the hard thing because it's right.
I know they'll make me laugh when I'm down
or move me beyond tears
I know they're only a click away with our 21st century gear.

I know I can simply open a book
or look them up online
and I know the reason they seem so great
Is because I see them through a lens.

And I know they don't even know me
And I know they don't even care
But when I hear some report
or a Twitter retort
or a photo of them on Instagram
when they speak on the news
or get lots of views
it brings me closer to them.

I can't help but feel
like my characters are real
and so that's why I chose
_____as my Idol 2016.

Adaora Elliott (14)

Weird But Wonderful

My idol is none other
Than my own somewhat crazy mother.
She's always there to lend a hand
And catches me when I land.
My idol also happens to be
My dad who believes he's in charge of me.
He's once again so true and kind
But needs to control his behind.
My idol also comes in the form
Of my little sis (so cute and warm).
Yes, she's annoying, that's very true
And yep, she does belong in a zoo.
My idol that is quite uncanny
Another family member, Grannie.
She built planes in the good old days
And seven children she had to raise.
My idol this time is plural
It's dancers that are professional.
They slave away to put on a show
The pain of which we can never know.
My idol next in line
Is someone who does not drink wine.
I despise all alcohol
So to that idea I do enthral.
My idol last and again not single,
Are people who're thoughtful and also bilingual.

They put in copious amounts of effort
To be and speak a language that's different.
I know my idols are many and strange
But dreams and wishes are in range.

Jodie Stone (13)

Idolise

Someone once asked me
Who do I idolise?
I don't think I gave them an answer then
And if they asked now I still wouldn't have one

I can't think of just one person
Who deserves that title
A person who helped shape me
Made me into who I am

I saw a girl cry one day
As a man gripped her wrist
Maybe a little too tight
And I decided I would never
Never let anyone have that sort of power
Over me, my emotions or my body
I think she'd be an idol of mine

One day I met an old couple
One half-blind - one could hardly walk
They told me of their regrets
No fulfilled dreams or expectations
They were incomplete

And I vowed to never let myself go like that
Work, work, work until my heart stopped
At least I would be satisfied

So I think my biggest idol is me
After all, it is me is it not
Who chooses what shapes myself
Where I go in life?

I am my own idol
I choose what shapes me
And I say that with pride.

Nour Tazaoui (14)

Grandma - My Inspiration

Whilst I have many idols,
There's one who's above the rest,
She's someone I admire,
Someone who is the best

She's someone who laughs,
Someone who cries,
Someone who loves
Through her very forgiving eyes

Whether it's digging in the garden,
Or cooking in the kitchen,
This very special lady
Is always happy to pitch in

She brings the family together,
She makes us all unite,
Long evenings at her house,
We dance into the night

Whilst she's dainty and fragile,
She's very strong inside,
For in her is a woman
Full of dignity and pride

Coming from Africa,
Anxious, scared and alone,
She strived to find a job
And bought a house on her own

Being a widower was not easy,
But it made her independent,
And I'm so glad that history
Makes me her descendant

To the most caring, kindest and loving woman I know,
Baa, I really do love you, more than words can show.

Nikisha Bhogaita (16)

Nathalia Romas - My Idol

N athalia Romas
A miable, adept and ambitious actress, simply like carrots and humus.
T alented Nathalia is half-Spanish and Australian, as well an American citizen
H er notorious saying: 'You can do it all' makes her a role model for children
A grin stretched across my heart, as soon as she astonished me with her skills.
L ike a ghost were her expressions, giving me the thrills.
I n the movie, the story would come to life as her eyes would flicker like a candle.
A ssiduous was Nathalia, but with her school and acting, how could she handle?

R oaring was her success in House of Anubis, her fans were kept near
O ccasionally moving to England showed determination towards her career
M any of her main messages state to follow your dreams,
A fter all this increases numerous amounts of young self esteems
S miles are found across the globe thanks to Nathalia, even in places like Somalia.

Yasmin Batoul Rafiq (12)

My Merciful Mother

When I'm feeling unloved or isolated,
She is always there to easily comfort me,
When fear slowly creeps up my icy cold spine,
Her warm, beautiful smile is always there to influence my tiny mouth
to turn my frown upside down,
When I am curled up all by myself in the stock cupboard,
waiting for somebody to notice my disappearance,
That calm, tender voice of hers chanting my name
always assures me that I am perfectly safe,
I know my eyes don't shine like emeralds, instead they look like mud,
I know she loves me for who I really am and could not ask for any more,
She thinks I'm unique in my very own way,
And I think the exact same about her,
This is because we are the exact same,
Mainly because she is my mother and I am her very own delicate and special baby,
And this is why she is my idol and I'm grateful that she is
because I want to be just like her when I'm a mother like she currently is.

Naomi Salumu Ngwewa (10)

A Poem For My Significant Person

I sometimes wish I could
Turn back time
Back to when
Everything
Was just fine
Back to when life was simple
And the little struggles were when I'd whine
Causing you to sing
To me softly
My very favourite and soothing lullabies
My first steps were just the beginning of my independence
My interaction with others
Was the starting bonds of understanding love and friendship
Our sudden outbursts and my tantrums
Were the things we quickly overcame and brought us closer
And the support after setbacks caused the epiphany of who loved me and did care
When others were absent and not there
And that they were shaping me from back then
Which led up to the present, right now, of the young, immature but happy teen I am now
And I'll hopefully do right and continue being happy until the end
Especially with you dear Mum. I love you so.

Cecile Kwarteng (12)

My Luckiest Mascot

The colour on my palette, the dollar in my wallet
Speeches given like Obama, causing White House level drama,
The champagne amongst the water, a stopper to my tears,
My personal human diary, from secret plans to fears

Someone to turn to; the catcher of dreams,
The bear hugs that follow, as perfect as it seems,
Someone who'll care; before, now and after
She holds her own culture and speaks the language of laughter

The teller of tales, her eyes: they hold stories,
From the scariest of nightmares to the midsummer fairies,
Above all is guidance, a most honest companion,
Through life and through problems, my gold-medal champion

Motherly love, brotherly protection,
As good as humans get, a most near-perfection,
Now please, hats off, to a time well-spent
And will spend on forever with my best friend!

Sabrina Priyanka Azmi (15)

My Family

Have I told you about a group?
The group who loves me.
This group is my family.
My family make me laugh,
My family make me smile,
My family like it when I dance,
Whenever I'm down,
They're always there for me.
And whenever they're down,
I'm always there for them.
Sometimes I pull a prank on them,
Sometimes they pull a prank on me,
We enjoy being a family
Sometimes I even paint a portrait of the family.
Or a volcano,
Or a butterfly,
They love all my paintings,
And they're always happy,
That I finish my homework on time,
My brother is so organised,
I wish I was like him.
But since we are all a family,
It's worth a try,
But they adore me no matter what!

Have I told you about a group?
The group who love me.
This group is my family.
My family make me laugh,
My family make me smile,
My family like it when I dance.

Urooj Rahimi (9)

For Bhaijan - I Miss You X

Everything I say is true,
Bhaijan, if you are reading this,
It's for you.
My brother is my second parent,
Always there, never distant.
He would help me get to sleep,
Hold me when I weep.
He was there for me in the bad times,
And was with me in my prime.
But I look up to him the most.
Confident and never an idle boast.
He is so smart in my eyes,
Hard-working and he always tries,
I guess I didn't appreciate it until he left.
When both of us cleft,
I wanted to write,
But that thought filled me with fright,
Because I wouldn't be talking to him.
And everything just went dim.
But then I remember the times,
When he taught me about enzymes,
Said goodnight at bedtimes.
And even maybe sometimes
He would let me sing
To his guitar, he would bring.
And even though I sounded dreadful,
And I knew after I would be regretful,
He still made me feel special.

Lana Masood Ahmed (13)

Who Do I Idolise?

The idol of my choice is tipping over my tongue,
It was so hard but I had to choose one.
A peculiar question you may settle upon,
A poem of which could produce a song.
Many people wonder who I love the most,
I don't like to boast.
A decision one shouldn't have to make,
But when my brother is not around, my life is at stake.
Jaden, you are my hero,
I've known you since the age of zero.
When you were born,
My heart was torn.
I love both of my brothers,
Even though they have different mothers.
But if I had to choose one,
It would be my brother; Charlotte's son.
I dread to think the worst of what without them the world would be like,
Jaden, I love you more than my quad bike.
I love Jaden and you cannot take away,
The love and friendship we made that day.

Ella-Rose Mulcare (16)

My Parents

Who do I idolise?
Is there anyone I symbolise?
They are my dynamite,
Lighting up the day and sky,
And my every night.

I see them in my dreams.
I see them when I am fast asleep.
They make my days complete.
They comfort me when I weep.
Without them, who would I be...

When it's time to pay the debt,
I shall render with no regret.
For once I was as helpless as thee
But they are those who helped me
To whom I owe my life to with glee.

They are my foundation,
They were with me for my life's duration
They will support me at my graduation
They have shown me my home nation
For they are my blood relation.

They are the makers of my appearance
My whole life has been in their presence
They have shown me a load of tolerance
They have worked with lots of endurance
For they are my parents

Faizah Hussain (11)

Reasons To Stay Alive

Shining light on a world that dare few talk about
You compose symphonies from death
You are resplendent
You are powerful enough to make your own ink run down the page
In the most sombre of times, you bring comfort
For many, you are medication
For a while, you eradicate the pain
To those who think that happiness is a faded photograph
You give hope
Like a mother's arms
You give the protection of steel armour
Who knew that so much could be derived from merely 200 pages?
Every word screams out a story
No man hears the same scream as the next
They all have their own idiosyncratic interpretations
You are compassionate
You are your own world
You are a lifesaver.

Chloe Chuck (14)

David Walliams

He's funny,
He's a comedian,
He's strict,
He's an author,
Round of applause to David Walliams!

You can't imagine someone like him,
Do you think he goes to the gym?
He's like a bunny,
Because he is funny,
Round of applause to David Walliams!

He must be muddled up,
As he is an author at the same time a comedian,
You must like this author,
If you don't like authors, you must like comedians,
Round of applause to David Walliams!

He always makes us laugh,
He is definitely better than a half,
I like his books,
And his looks,
Round of applause to David Walliams!

He's an author,
He's a comedian,
Round of applause to David Walliams!

Zineb Ait Ziane (9)

Always Be My King

Dads love and dads care,
Fathers are different.
They're the ones who truly want to be there,
Dads are special but fathers are different.

Fathers are nice and fathers are kind,
But whose father is also their best friend?
Father best friends are hard to find,
There through thick and thin till the end.

Father best friends are cool and father best friends are fun,
But is this best friend your loyal king?
Loyal kings are the special one,
Love, defence, loyalty and affection they bring.

My dad consists of all of these,
My first love, my idol king.
Even when I meet my prince,
Daddy, you'll always be my king.

Shannon Rose Byrne (15)

My Favourite Person Is My Dad

I am so glad,
he is my dad.
I am very proud,
because I am his child.
My dad is working pretty,
he is taking me to the city.
He takes care of me,
my sister and my mum.
Always he buys me whatever I want,
and he never misses whatever I want to do.
I give my thousand kisses to my dad,
he cooks my favourite food,
it is really good.
He takes me in his car,
even if it is very far.
He loves me so much,
so I do not make trouble too much.
He looks after my family,
he teaches me good habits.
He expects me to be a good boy,
I give respect to him always.
My dad is my role model,
he is very best in this whole world.
I want his love always,
because he is very special to me.
I love my dad,
I am never sad.
I say thank you God for my dad.

Dathusan Thavaneswaran (6)

My Poetry Idol: My Sister

My sister is kind, my sister is cool.
My sister is there when I've had a bad day at school.
My sister achieves, she reaches her goals.
She does her best and into her work she puts her heart and soul.
She inspires me and says that I could do anything I want to.
She helps me and advises me and I believe what she says is true.
She teaches me to take any chances and drop any fears,
To get past hard obstacles and not let anything bring tears.
She teaches me to never give up and work hard to achieve my dreams.
To learn everything I can, no matter how hard things may seem.
She teaches me that you should always let hope triumph over doubt.
That from every seed, a beautiful flower will sprout.

Jessica Nelson (12)

Dear Boris Johnson

I tribute you only this:
A thesaurus of praises
For the bringer of bliss
For him, who amazes.

None may ever mislead him.
Voice that commands a nation
to vote for the 'freedom'
that led to cessation.
To 'take back control' of some
borders that so angered crowds.
Remove those who come from
outside, back to the clouds.
You have been stabbed in the back
by the treacherous Michael.
No fear! That sad attack
will not break your cycle,

but revive your big brain's
referendum remains.

I admire you greatly;
Your oh-so-bombastic courage.
You're responsible for it.
So does Brexit mean Brexit?

Romer Palad (16)

Shakespeare My Role Model

Listen carefully and listen clear
Lend me your ears
And I will tell you a story about
My role model, Shakespeare
Who wrote poems that made us happy or made us fear
He was born in 1564
That day he was smarter than us all
A role model who was great
And he had much to debate
Here are some of my favourite books
Othello, a dreadful scene
But interesting it seems
Hamlet, a bloodthirsty book
But one life was all it took
The Taming of the Shrew
That didn't make me go boo!
Shakespeare should be a role model to us all
For he made the best poets that will never fall.

Carmel Temilore Oniye (10)

Malala Yousafzai

Recently I read a book
About a girl who fought for her education
She got shot
And stole the hearts of the nation

Her name was Malala
She went to Khushal Public School
It was run by her father
Who was no fool

He knew the dangers of the terrorists
But continued the girls' teaching
He thought no matter your sex
Your dreams are worth reaching

You have a right
Like we all do
No matter what sex or race
Christian or Hindu

She's won countless prizes
For speaking her mind
She's continued her learning
Much more than was assigned

Malala Yousafzai
A girl who fought for her education
She got shot
And stole the hearts of the nation.

Koryn Archer (10)

Poetry Idol

Shaz, my aunty, is my Poetry Idol.
Shaz is my favourite person in the whole wide world because she is very kind,
she loves me a lot, she always takes me out to my favourite restaurants
and she takes me on amazing, adventurous holidays around the world.

- **A** lways awesome
- **U** nderstanding
- **N** utty and fun
- **T** akes care of me and everyone
- **Y** ummy food we both love to eat

- **S** mart and smiling all the time
- **H** eart of gold
- **A** mazing and adventurous
- **Z** ooming me around to explore the world

Just want to tell you Shaz, that you are my favourite one!

Aaria Bains (6)

Grandfather, I Miss You

You always have time to listen,
when everyone else is busy,
And you know all the answers,
To the questions I ask.
I know it hurt you;
It hurt me too,
but now that you are gone,
All I know is I miss you.
you were there for so long,
I never thought you would leave,
I thought you had another year,
Waiting up your sleeve.
I might be a bit selfish,
But I wish you were here,
Or if you stayed,
For one more year.
I just want to tell you,
That you're always in my heart,
Even though I didn't get to see you,
I know that we're not apart.

Rishika Raghunandanan (12)

My Mummy

My mummy you're the best
You showed me how to dress
You teach me new games and tricks
When I'm good you give me lots of treats

My mummy is special
Under your protection
She gives me delicious meals
That fill me full and filled
You teach me more things to learn
And teach my siblings too
You take us out for pleasure
And leisure on weekends

You showed me how to read and write
You always read to us at night
You make us read and write alright
And always do our homework right

You are the best mother of all
You are always there for us all
Thank you for the thing that you've done for me
I love you and you love me.

Prince Opara (10)

My Idol!

My idol is my dad
because he saves people and gets hurt for people.
My dad is a police officer
he is strong and brave.
He keeps people safe like all other police officers do.
Once he came home with a black eye
but still worked the next day.
It is not just that, when we went to Italy he badly bruised his foot
but kept walking.
As well, a little toddler was walking in front of his mother
and my dad had already crossed the road
but the toddler was on the road and a car came
so my dad got the toddler and put him on the path.

So that is why my dad is my idol!

Megan Williams (9)

My Idol Is...

M y idol is an artist and very smart
Y es, he has a way to a person's heart

B ecause he's special
R eally, all teachers know him
O ver the moon he is
T o be able to draw is his passion
H is levels are great
E veryone in my school knows
R eal, his drawings are

G iving is also why I like him
L oving is why he's my idol
O f course makes me smile
D rawings are batteries to the remote to his life
I dol is the word when I think of him

My idol is... My brother Glodi!

Jocelyn Ngomabie (10)

My One And Only Best Friend

You're strong, you're beautiful, you're kind, you're funny.
You're always there when I need you whether you want to be or not.
You're always pretending you're fine,
so you worry me not.

You can always see through me and know when something's up,
you never get angry at me or upset when I do something wrong
and for that reason you make me strong.

You are my best friend, you belong in my heart,
We go through ups and downs, but still nothing can tear us apart.

For those reasons you inspire me.

Ashley James (14)

Super Mom To The Rescue

I come home filled with despair
but she is always there
with her superpower of hope,
She gives me lectures and jokes
that tickle my stomach
and turns my frown to a smile,
She is always the one who I use as a pillow
for when I cry like a weeping willow,
She is always my hero
who takes all the diseases
and viruses stored inside of me,
Her with her super power.

Every day I awake
and see the shining sun
in front of my eyes
and as I have a glance,
This smile of hers
gives me the energy to look forward to my daily life,
She gives me power
because she is my hero
My super mom hero.

Satiya Yaya (14)

My Idol

There when the skies are grey
There on a dark day
There when I'm feeling blue
And I will always be there for you
You help me when I'm feeling ill
And I don't know anyone else with the talent, the skill
Always so patient, so kind
When I'm worried, you help me clear my mind
I know I don't say this as much as I should
If I could just be with you I would
Because you're the sun to my dark sky
Just writing this brings a tear to my eye
And I will be with you till the day I die
Because you're the apple to my pie
I love you Mum
I always have
And I always will.

Maddi Davis (12)

Fading Away

I will always remember her eyes, how she smiled,
her eyes like stars glowing in the sky.
I will always remember her cheeks popping out like springs.
My memories of her peacefully playing piano
or eating chocolate covered biscuits.
Her house was small and musty,
She sat in her chair like a queen in her throne.
One day she flew away like a butterfly flapping.
I felt like I had lost a part of me, like my leg.
I look out of the window, believing she will come back one day.
I've lost important memories of us,
they are slipping away like the tears from my eyes.

Oliver Poole (8)

Friend Idols

They show me the right way,
They always help me every day,
Care for me when I am sad,
Tell me the truth when my writing is bad.
Keep me in the zone,
Make me feel never alone,
Feelings that give me ideas,
Like what they feel like they are scared of gorillas.
My friends are the best idols,
That's why I'm giving them this title,
My friends are the best,
I couldn't want any of the rest.

I want to mention my friends -
Friends from primary,
Friends from football team Blodmere Falcons,
Football coach,
Friends from secondary.

Georgia Anne Ellis (12)

My Poetry Idol; Mum Rocks This Town

I idolise my mum, for different laws
Mum also has no flaws
If she did I'd eat my hat!

Mum tries to make everything fair
Even if my sis breaks a chair
Which wouldn't even make her oh so mad
If I started to drift off and daydream
It wouldn't make her go a glamorous green
She would just ask me, if I could kindly clean the kitchen!

Just to add, my mum's got the best singing voice ever
And she sings her heart out always and forever
She is the coolest, kindest, best mum in the world!

Paavun Kaur (9)

If I Could Catch A Dream

If I could catch a dream,
Happiness would spread,
Wars would stop and everyone
Would smile and dance instead.

If I could catch a dream,
My writing would be read by
Children of all ages,
My heart would soar if they
Just longed to turn the pages.

If I could catch a dream,
Poaching would immediately stop.
All animals would be free to
Swim, walk, fly or hop.

If I could catch a dream,
Life would be eternally magic,
Everyone would sport a friendly grin, and
Nothing would be tragic.

If I could catch a dream...

Katie Muckells (10)

A Hurricane

She's a silent hurricane
A storm without rain
Without her love you'll never be the same

Say you can't trust her
She's got a sinister smile
Her wicked lips torture you
You wonder what they'll say

She doesn't have a brain, it won't matter anyway
Her brain is long gone, dead as can be
When she does speak it's useless
Quieter than me
Less than a whisper
Smaller than a mouse

She's still a hurricane though she just doesn't move her mouth!

Jasmine Lily Bloor (12)

Happiness

Nothing more, nothing less,

than future success,
keeping me alive,
making me strive,
to live outside my head,
and be more than what they said.
Even when you fall apart,
a perfect piece of art,
a beautiful mess,

nothing more, nothing less,

than pure kindness,
if cracked, never broken,
anger controlled, not spoken,
people push and shove,
you show them love.
An inspiration to me,
I just wish you could see,
you're nothing more, nothing less,
than my source of happiness.

Mya Coco-Bassey (14)

My Mum

She struts like a supermodel
I just wanna have a cuddle.
She makes me feel like a majestic princess
But at home she says, 'Rinse this.'
I love her so much I can't explain it
It's speechless.
I don't know how she does it but I can say...

You are my best friend forever
I just wanna stay with you
Forever!
You are my other half, my soul and body
I can tell you anything, even when I'm stroppy
I wanna be like you, my human copy
You mean the world to me and I wanna say again...

Rashidah Ajayi (10)

I Love You

The couples that are meant to be,
Are the ones who go through everything that tear them apart,
But become stronger.

That's why I'd rather have bad times with you,
than good times with someone else.
I'd rather be beside you in an apocalypse
than be safe and warm by myself.
I'd rather have hard times together,
than have it easy alone.
I'd rather have the one,
that holds the key to my heart

That's why I will love you,
to the very end.
You are not a person,
you are my friend.

Tanica Cherelle Karen Anderson (13)

My Cousin, My Best Friend

Something that everyone in our family knows,
You and I, have always been close.
Got along through all those years,
Many joys and many tears.
A special cousin and dearest friend,
My deepest appreciation I wish to send.
You've always stood by my side,
When I lost, you were my guide.
The bond we share, to me is dear,
When we're together, I have no fear.
Sometimes, I bother and even annoy,
A special cousin, that brings so much joy.

Thaila Smith (12)

The Echo Of A Voice

My idol isn't someone who can be defined
By a name or a gender
By a smile or a job
My idol is someone who enjoys what they do
Someone who wakes up every morning and can't wait to get the day started
Because their job makes them happy
Someone who truly believes that their voice is making a difference
Even if only a small one
Whether it's a builder or a singer,
an actor or an artist
If they're working every day to make their voice heard
They will always be an idol in my mind.

Sophie Rea (13)

I Want To Be Like My Mummy

My name is Nimrah
I want to be like my mummy.
It is hard work to be like my mummy.
If I want to be like my mummy I have to help my mummy.
If I want to be like my mummy I have to copy my mummy.
If my mummy is unwell I can help my mummy
like when my mummy does for me.
If my mummy went on holiday I could help my mummy with the suitcase
and on the way back.
I have the best mum in the whole universe.
I love my mummy a lot.

Nimrah Jan (7)

All My Idols

My miracle mum,
Is number one,
She is always there,
Even when I'm in tears.

My fabulous friends,
Are always on trend,
We're together forever,
We never say never.

Jacqueline Wilson,
The greatest writer ever,
You can read her books wherever,
As it inspires everywhere.

All of these together,
Is what I idolise,
And want to be,
When I am older and free.

Samerah Khan Bi (11)

Pip's Poem

Brave and strong,
But yet so gentle.
Full of fight.
Her love is instrumental
In melting the hardest of human hearts.
She fought for her life,
She won that battle.
Full of determination.
Through her trials and strife,
She made us stronger.

People moan about their life,
She smiles and lives a better world in her head.
She sings soft songs,
She makes your heart melt.
No one is like her.
She is a miracle from up above.
An angel sent down to bring us love.

Hannah Forster (12)

Role Model

You look around, you see people happy, sad, mad, all different emotions
But who or what inspires them to be unique, individual
One of a kind you might say
The person who inspires me is happy, loving, unique
And follows her dreams
Her name is Jacqueline Wilson
She has inspired me to be free, individual and to follow my dreams
Also to become an author
That's my role model, who's yours?

Anya Linda Kozlowski (10)

My Genial Grandad

G randad, you are my rock,
R adiating your love around your grandchildren,
A lways protecting us and keeping us happy.
N othing can compare to the pure kindness that pours out of your heart,
D elicious sweets that you give us every day,
A ssortments of herbals and Skittles, just as sweet as you.
D elight will always surround us when you are with us.

Rimsha Shoukat (17)

The Loves Of My Life

The Lord is my creator and provider.
My mother is my bearer.
My father is my carer.
My sister is my friend.
My brother is my protector.
My grandmother is my helper.
My grandfather is my problem solver.
My uncle is my saviour.
My aunt is my trust.
My husband is my other half.
My wife is my better half.
My friend is a shoulder to cry on.
My son is my wealth.
My daughter is my jewel.

Shazia Rahman (15)

My Dad Is My Idol

My dad is my idol
I love my dad, he's so brave, tough and fearless
I love his hugs and kisses,
I love when he tucks me up and kisses me goodnight
He makes sure the bed bugs don't bite,
I love our family days out, we laugh and shout,
My dad is my dad and I love him so
He's my idol and I want him to know.

Charley Anders (7)

Mum

Loads of people idolise their mum
Mine's a bit of fun
She has been through a lot
Never to be sad just trot on she said
I'm always here
Whenever you need an ear
From a lung transplant to a horrific disease
You have stayed strong
I love you, Mum
Stay strong and have some fun!

Misty Worofka (13)

Best Friend

The one I ask for advice,
The one I tell my deepest secrets to,
The person I keep close to my heart when times get tough,
The person who keeps me going after a heartbreak.

Not everyone can have a person like you,
But I'm the one who needs you the most.

Tayla Alison Schofield (13)

Granddad

G randdad is epic at football
R eally likes Arsenal FC
A llotment shop is his call and a
N ice cup of coffee
D oes coin and stamp collecting
D oes fish and chip sleepovers
A lways likes long walking
D efinitely watches Colchester over and over.

Jack Mascot (9)

My Mummy Is My Idol

My mummy's got big eyes,
so she can see me very well.
My mummy's got big ears,
so she can hear me very well.

My mummy's got big arms,
so she can cuddle me a lot.
My mummy's got a big heart
so she can love me a lot.

Sithija Kurukulasuriya (5)

My Mother

L ovely mummy, as beautiful as a princess.
O utstanding mum as a scientist.
V ery loved, a lovely person.
E very mum is special.

Y oung mother, just a girl.
O ne in a million.
U seful mum as a working mum.

Ebubechukwu Chidubem Onwuzurigbo (8)

Who I Idolise

I idolise not a pop star or a footballer,
not the Queen or the Prime Minister,
in fact it's an author,
JK Rowling,
in my opinion the best author,
who writes Harry Potter,
Friendship and fantasy,
wizards and witches,
how she thinks of it...

Lina Jabeen (10)

Happy Helpful Hermione

Happy, helpful Hermione
Helping all around
Hooray, hooray, hooray for that
Happy, helpful Hermione
She's as clever as old folk
Hooray, hooray, hooray for that
Happy, helpful Hermione.

Veronika Andersone (11)

Ode To A Chocolate Digestive

I love you, chocolate digestive
You mean so much to me
So please, be kind
Don't snap in two
When I dunk you in my tea!

Connie Power

The Natural World

To David Attenborough, who's four score and ten,
And to Steve Backshall, who's born who knows when!
You have opened my eyes to the natural world,
Ever since I was a very little girl.

From blue whales to bullet ants,
Chasing tuna fish, Steve lost his pants.
Spectacled caimans and manta rays.
Blue ringed octopi and ospreys.

Lacewings, mambas and gorillas.
Irukandji jellyfish in Australia.
Tarantula hawk wasps and indri,
Spitting cobra and sea anemone.

Giant millipedes and dragonflies,
Bushbabies with massive eyes.
Lemurs, bats and scorpions,
Komodo dragons and leaf chameleons.

I thank you for inspiring me,
Through the magic of my TV.

Atira Todd (10)
Bamford Academy, Rochdale

Hermione Granger

Me and Hermione both have
A love for reading which is so huge.
We prefer not to break the rules
But people judge us harshly.

Me and Hermione both have
People thinking we're strange.
We're smart and follow the rules
But people judge us harshly.

Me and Hermione both have
People who are mean to us.
You don't have to like us
But people judge us harshly.

Me and Hermione both have
People who don't talk to us.
Look inside us and see we're not geeks
But people judge us harshly.

Hermione is my hero
A girl who loves to read.
She helped me to understand
That I'm fantastic as I am!

Isabelle Baker (10)
Bamford Academy, Rochdale

Esme Baker Gardon

Esme Baker Gardon
Has a thing for saying pardon.
She is ten years of age
And always lets the dog out of the cage.

Esme Baker Gardon
Has always shone
She loves eating veg
And leaving the lights on.

Esme Baker Gardon
Has a friend called Alley John
Has black spots on her face
And is very curious.

Esme Baker Gardon
Loves to have barbecues 'n' jump
She always says, 'Hey'
Esme Baker Gardon.

Daisy Parton (10)
Bamford Academy, Rochdale

My Mum

She always has the brightest smile,
The good thing is it lasts for a while.
My mum won't think, she'll just do,
And she will always love me too.

She'll find the positive in everything,
Her smile will pay for a diamond ring,
She loves me and I know it,
She'll do anything not to blow it.

Laila Kaysor (10)
Bamford Academy, Rochdale

Miss Darby

M aking children feel happy
I nteresting
S uper awesome
S aying kind words to us

D ancing to music
A mazing at work
R acing with me
B ut she is the coolest
Y es, she is the best teacher.

Amber Aslam (7)
Bamford Academy, Rochdale

My Mummy

M y favourite person is my mummy
U nless she doesn't give me a dummy.
M y mummy always tells me funny jokes
M y mummy also thinks it's funny
Y ummy Jummy she always calls me and I don't think it's funny.

Haniya Arien (6)
Bamford Academy, Rochdale

My Brother, Joshua

Happy, happy,
Is the young boy who never wears a nappy.

Friend, friend,
Even though he drives me round the bend.

Funny, funny,
When he asks me for some money.

Caring, caring,
When he goes around sharing.

Harry Hoyle (10)
Bamford Academy, Rochdale

Mummy

M y mummy is the best.
U ses her money when she goes to Tesco.
M y mummy takes me to Tesco every morning.
M y mummy gets me crisps.
Y ou are the best mummy in the world.

Aleeza Azam (7)
Bamford Academy, Rochdale

My Sister

My little sister Lily
Is very, very silly.
She draws on walls
In the halls.
She puts her plate
On her face and her mum says, 'What a state!'

Charlie James Magnall (7)
Bamford Academy, Rochdale

Beliefs

Strong and determined.
Fought greatly for their beliefs.
Enthusiastic
Equal rights for all women.
Suffragettes gave me a vote.

Esme Coulton
Bamford Academy, Rochdale

My Mum

Awesome, cool, super
My mum is wonderfully
Super, cool, awesome
Caring, kind, loving
My mum is wonderfully
Caring, kind, loving.

Joseph Samuel Thomas (9)
Bamford Academy, Rochdale

Maira

M y best friend
A mazing at work
I nteresting
R acing me
A wesome because she is my best friend.

Aisha Khawaja (7)
Bamford Academy, Rochdale

My Hero

People say you don't have to fly to be a superhero, but mine does.
They soar through the stratosphere,
Beyond the moon and the stars,
Zooming through galaxies and skidding past black holes.

My hero appears at certain times,
When I'm worried or when I'm upset.
Mostly when I'm bored and have nothing to do.
They jump into my head,
And flick the switches of every lightbulb in my brain.

They dance like flamingoes,
Sifting their beaks through cool, fresh water from a desert oasis.
They wear the strangest of clothes;
Jumpers woven from unicorn hair,
Laced with fairy magic sparkles.
Thunder and lightning earrings,
Imbuing the immeasurable power of creativity.

Most people's heroes have an Achilles heel,
Which stops them dead in their tracks.
I have to admit; mine does too.
They can't do anything on their own,
But together, we are strong.
We can make anything happen.

My hero cannot be contained,
They can never be confined to a box.
Wherever you see them, they're outside the box, thinking.
Their ideas burst and spread colour everywhere,
Like a paint-filled balloon.

My hero is my imagination.
People say, 'Oh, it's just your imagination.'
That's like saying, 'Oh, it's just Superman.'

Hiba Waseem (12)
King Edward VI Handsworth School For Girls, Birmingham

Love For Eternity

I have always been told to say the facts,
However, many people don't follow this rule.
Some people may hesitate to tell the truth.
The truth of who their role model is.

Through them it was how I learnt how to walk.
Through them it was when I began to dream.
Through them it is how my aims just grow and grow.
Through them it is how I feel incredibly unique.

My role models are one of a kind.
Since the news of my arrival,
Till the breath that I am breathing now,
They have always been there to ignite a light on my way.

From the warmth of their embraces,
I feel so preserved from the harsh world outside,
And with their cosy comforting,
I know that I am invulnerable.

Every time someone says that I'm dumb,
They are always there to back me up.
No matter whether they are right or wrong,
They will always reassure me that my brain isn't numb.

If you could see deep into my heart,
You would be able to see the special place,
Where my role models reside,
And see the never-ending and eternal love for them.

Counting each sacrifice, that they have done for me,
Would probably take me years along with a few weeks.
Here draws the end, revealing my role models.
Yes, you were correct, my role models are my parents, my life!

Anika Sowan (12)
King Edward VI Handsworth School For Girls, Birmingham

Your Mum And Dad Will Always Be There

Nine months is a long wait for birth and when you get used to it,
You hate it when you're born.
Blinding lights in your face,
Being whisked away for measurements and such.
But when when you're placed in loving arms and company,
You know Mom and Dad will always be there for you.

Saying things like 'goo-goo' or 'ga-ga',
Is incredibly easy, but when you say, 'Mummy' or 'Daddy',
You know Mom and Dad will always be there for you.

When you see that new gadget,
But Mom says no,
Dad will follow and take care of his girls' needs,
Cause Dad will always be there for you.

When those growing up details,
Get too mushy and awkward,
Mom sits there and makes everything comfortable,
You know Mom will always be there for you.

When you do that favourite sport,
And take a nasty fall and see those naughty cuts and grazes,
Dads will tell you his little princess doesn't give up.
And that's when you know Dad will always be there for you.

So when it comes to the time of marriage,
When Mom helps you find the dress of your dreams,
And when Dad takes you down the altar,
You know your parents will always be there for you,
No matter what.

Jaskeerat Kaur Gill (13)
King Edward VI Handsworth School For Girls, Birmingham

My Role Model

She's been famous since her birth,
I guess what could she do?
She's also not the first,
Her family's famous too!

She's stunning; she's a model,
She's been in tonnes of shoots,
For 'Cosmopolitan' and 'People',
Wearing lots of outfits and shoes!

You're probably wondering who she is,
Well I guess you'll have to wait,
Just like her audience...
When she turns up fashionably late!

Her life has been documented,
For many, many years,
She's grown up on the internet,
Surely the hate has brought her tears?

But she keeps calm and carries on,
Ignoring all that hate,
This is why she's my role model,
Although others may debate.

She has even explored beauty,
A real success she's had!
With her lip kits and eye shadows,
I'm sure there'll be more to add!

he travels far and wide,
To exotic, scenic islands,
Although she is not always relaxing,
She travels to foster homes in the highlands!

She is Kylie Jenner of course!
She's so nice and kind,
Her Snapchats keep me updated
People like her are hard to find!

Holly Wiseman (12)
King Edward VI Handsworth School For Girls, Birmingham

My Idol's Name Is Anonymous...

My idol's name is Anonymous,
They are not famous and would not like to be seen,
So keep it a secret - shhh!
We can't get in the way of her good deeds,
She only speaks when someone's life's in danger,
It's her life's domain,
She lurks in the corner,
And she's far from a saint,
She slaves all day for a cup of tea,
To keep a roof over her head,
And even when the world's not in her favour,
She'll make life for her children before she's dead,

My idol's name is Anonymous,
They are not famous and would not like to be seen,
So keep it a secret - shh!
We can't get in the way of his good deeds,
From my own experience - I have seen,
A terrifying guy - a 'gangster' even,
Who is thought to be mean,
He'll go out of his way to help somebody,
Even an old lady who can't go her own way,
It's just the way he looks,
It doesn't determine what he says,

My idol's name is Anonymous,
They are not famous and would not like to be seen,
So keep it a secret - shhh!
We can't get in the way of their amazing deeds.

Esha Din (12)
King Edward VI Handsworth School For Girls, Birmingham

My Cat Mittens

I love my dear cat, Mittens, and everything about her,
I always love to feed her cat food and stroke her soft, beautiful fur.
Her beauty always seems to mesmerise me:
With her white, snowy fur with black and ginger spots,
Her big, black tail and emerald eyes,
It really is a sight you really cannot deny!
If only the inside of her was as beautiful as the outside...

She is extremely territorial, with no friends at all.
Although there is one kitten that tries to play but ends with both of them having a brawl.
She scratches me every time I give her a stroke, I ask, 'Why, Mittens, why?'
But only gives a vexed miaow and glares at me like I'm some joke.

She sleeps 24/7, barely being awake,
Every time I try to play with her,
Her face just screams, 'Waking up was a mistake!'

Everywhere she walks, she seems to leave a trail of white fur,
Furniture, clothes, rugs, you name it,
It always just results in me using the lint roller.

But despite all these crazy things (and many, many more),
I will always love Mittens,
The cat that I adore.

Nadine Bowie-Fox (12)
King Edward VI Handsworth School For Girls, Birmingham

Bethany Leigh Jordan

The title is 'Bethany Leigh Jordan',
You may not know who she is.
She's not Michelle Obama and her videos don't lead to boredom.
A large following yet only a young age: sixteen,
She calls her fans, 'My Human Beans!'

Her personality is as bubbly as that character in Dumb Ways to
Die that drank out of date medicine,
And her looks are as gorgeous as Ariana Grande.
She isn't one to make a careless sin,
She thinks before her actions.

Not only does she love her 'Bethsties',
We pop onto Instagram and double tap her selfies
To make sure she interacts with her fans,
She does several live streams monthly.

Oh no! I've left out one bit,
You'd think she's busy with her job, correct?
However, she takes time out of her day to see people who
support her.

The title is 'Bethany Leigh Jordan',
You may not know who she is.
But she means the world to me,
And I know who she is.

Sophie Dang (13)
King Edward VI Handsworth School For Girls, Birmingham

My Hero

A flame can burn, even with the slightest spark
An equation can be completed, with just an equals sign
But what about courage?
Is it easy to find?
Or hard to maintain?
But what about a strong mentality?
Is it easy to have one?
Or hard to use it?
But what about fear?
Is it easy to gain?
Or hard to overcome?
Even all elements know resilience and perseverance is the key to succeed,
And so does my hero
In her life, 'fear' is the only surrounding habitat
The only obstacle to survive
The only item shattering hopes
There, she lights up the everlasting shadow
Just like the night sky, with a star shining amongst the darkness
Courage is her only ally
Her name is Lawrence...
Jennifer Lawrence
This is my hero
This is my hero, strong and beautiful

This is my hero, strong and beautiful, a league of her own
And that's what makes her my hero
She is a lioness, powerful and free.
She is my hero, strong and beautiful.

Maariya Khan (13)
King Edward VI Handsworth School For Girls, Birmingham

Who Is Important?

When I am alone,
She is by my side,
She looks after me every day.

When I need help,
She is there right away,
Always there to fulfil my needs.

If I have any worries,
She irons them out,
Of nothing I must fret.

She is by my side,
All the time,
The bravest woman I know.

Mamma, I love you,
I will love you forever,
More than you could ever know.

My papá is there,
Whenever I need him,
Nothing gets in his way.

He works so hard,
To ensure that I have,
The best possible life.

He lights up my life,
Like the bright, resilient sun,
There is nothing he can't do.

Whenever there are any doubts,
No matter what they may be,
With my papá, they scatter away.

He shines a light on my darkness,
He is the sun to my moon,
I love him more than anything.

Rebecca Sofia Middleton (13)
King Edward VI Handsworth School For Girls, Birmingham

A True Hero

Who is my hero?
Who could it be?
Is it you?
Maybe me?

Tough or weak,
Large or petite,
Confident or shy,
Horrid or polite.

My hero must have purpose,
Trustworthy, that's for sure,
Must always have a gentle smile,
Definitely not something vile.

They should be nice,
Like read you a book,
That clearly isn't Captain Hook.

It isn't someone with a whole load of fame,
But I do certainly know their name.

They led me,
They fed me,
They hugged me,
Kept me warm.

They laughed with me,
They laughed with me,
Jumped around all day,
Even in the darkest times they made me
Shout, '*Hooray*!'

Did you guess,
To find out my hero's name
Time to know who they are called,
I'll say it quickly so you don't get bored:
My ultra cool mother - Mum!

Madleen Mohammad (12)
King Edward VI Handsworth School For Girls, Birmingham

My Hero

Stupendous and spectacular, she has been called many things,
She arises me at the break of dawn,
With the light that she brings.

Glistening and gleaming she shines in every way,
Whenever it is raining,
She is there to save the day.

Phenomenal and precious, her face is so divine,
She captures everyone's thoughts,
Oh how I wish she was mine.

Beaming and beautiful, she clearly stands out,
Gowned in a delicate yellow garment,
She is the fairest without a doubt.

Joyous and jubilant, she guides us through the day,
She shines on the radiant flowers,
Especially during the holy month of May.

Incandescent and individual, she reigns in the sky,
No wonder is that,
Who would ever ask why?

Loving and loyal, we are eventually forced to part,
I wish to stay with her,
Although she must leave when it is dark.

Mary Hoggard (13)
King Edward VI Handsworth School For Girls, Birmingham

My Idol

She is the queen of pop,
She is always at the top,
She is the queen of style,
And yes, she has been in the music industry for a while,
But sometimes as a person she isn't the best behaved,
Yet her legs always look like they have just been shaved,
Yes, you might have guessed,
The person in my opinion is the best,
Her name is Beyoncé Knowles
She brings happiness to people's souls,
She is married to Jay-Z,
Their daughter is called Blue-Ivy,
They are the ultimate power couple you see,
She still is the best person to me,
The music she makes,
From me the breath it takes,
Beyoncé's music is meaningful,
Beyoncé's lyrics are powerful,
She always lights you up when you're down,
Upside down she turns that frown,
To conclude, her music makes me feel confident,
Beyoncé inspires me to be different.

Simran Nandhra (12)
King Edward VI Handsworth School For Girls, Birmingham

Maddie Ziegler

Perfection, does such thing exist?
If it did there would be no other place for it but this,
A dance so majestic, so gripping,
The whole nation is in silence,
For five years she was viewed in 130 countries,
Now has branched out to more,
Perfection is her dancing,
Tranquil and serene,
She holds the burden of upholding her image,
Smiling bravely, not revealing,
The stress she faces every day,
At just 14 years of age,
Courage comes in more forms than one,
Dancing, performing, acting,
Most importantly however,
Standing up for what she believes in,
Doing the Livvy and supporting ALS,
Silently supporting her fans,
She may not realise the effect she has on them,
But the impact is phenomenal,
Madison Ziegler is her name,
Courage, confidence and helping is her game.

Safaa Arooj Taj (12)
King Edward VI Handsworth School For Girls, Birmingham

My Hairo!

I have many heroes,
All bold and brave,
They've travelled the world - you see,
But they are all close to me,
However,
The one I choose to write about,
Cannot be compared to a large amount,
It is in my mind,
All the time,
Day and night,
My hero gets rid of my knots,
And - trust me - there are lots,
My hero is my hairbrush,
It travels through the tangles of my hair,
It makes it feel lush,
It combs away my fears,
It gets right behind my ears,
I know,
It seems quite daft - indeed,
At least it's not something pathetic - like weed!
I have many heroes,
Such as my mother or brother,
But my hairbrush is just right,
To create a poem about,
And that is that - my poem is done!
My hero is my hairbrush - that's it!

Harneek Sandhu (12)
King Edward VI Handsworth School For Girls, Birmingham

My Hero

My hero isn't a superhero,
My hero isn't a powerful creature,
In fact my hero isn't even famous.

My hero is super,
My hero is powerful,
And my hero is famous to me.

Unlike other heroes,
My hero doesn't fly,
Nor does he have powers.

Unlike other heroes,
My hero talks to all,
Not only when they're in trouble.

In simple words,
My hero is remarkable,
Better than Superman or Batman.

In simple words,
My hero is tremendous,
Better than Spider-Man or Captain America.

I will tell you who my hero is,
He may not be a hero to you,
But he is to me.

I will tell you who my hero is,
He may not be a hero to you,
But my hero is my dad.

Visvesa Modi (13)
King Edward VI Handsworth School For Girls, Birmingham

My Unknown Smile

He's someone who faced misery for years,
I only started,
He lost someone beloved, once, and then again,
I only started.
His brother disappeared: no reason been told
My sister... dying and I know why...
Yet when we found his brother, he smiled,
Even after all the agonising pain.
He stayed expectant,
Just like I need to.
Hopeful and wait for that unknown smile,
That he had, to appear for me.
The two lost twins,
Three desperate sisters.
Waiting to be brought that happiness.
He may not be real but he made me happy,
Along with my heart.
He keeps me up from being where my sister is.
He's my unknown smile,
Keeping that unknown mask on my face,
With an unknown smile,
Waiting to be true.
Just like his.

Uzma Amin (13)
King Edward VI Handsworth School For Girls, Birmingham

I Bet You Haven't Heard This One Yet

My role model may be the oddest one yet,
But you will agree with me on this I bet,
Warmth, cosiness and comfort,
Those words occur to me without any effort.

Though sometimes it may be a struggle,
Making me feel very dull,
Blinded by the sun's rays,
Just makes me want to spend more time to laze.

But I can't spend all my time with it,
But I do have to admit,
That with it I spend half my day,
And all I want to do is just stay.

My duvet snuggles me tight,
Helping me get through the night,
My role model is my bed,
And no I haven't hit my head.

My role model may have been the oddest one yet,
But you would have agreed with me on this, this I bet!

Jerusha Jeyasuthan (12)
King Edward VI Handsworth School For Girls, Birmingham

My Idols Are Fictional

In times of daunting peril,
They have power in their bones.

They are borne from pen and paper,
Ink runs through their veins, like blood.
Composed from words,
Just strokes on pages,
Their lives - little by little - are built up.

The tales they tell aren't
Always simple.
So much more than a
Love or a loss.
Tales of courage and cowardice
Lies and the truth.

The battles they face are disheartening,
Yet they always (somehow) struggle through.
They will sacrifice so much
For the sake of a friend,
Risk themselves
For the greater good.

They can influence so much
through the stories they tell
They are my heroes - Absolute.

Gursimran Kaur (12)
King Edward VI Handsworth School For Girls, Birmingham

Mother

My role model is based on the leaves,
How they flow gently in the breeze,
It's everywhere around you hidden in disguise,
It comforts you and it tries,
To keep up with all of your sighs,
It is interesting and colourful,
Also reposing if you're stressful,
You kill it yet you want to save it,
It supplies your needs,
It is made from the seeds,
Mother Nature is its name,
Inspirational is what gets it its fame,
Mother Nature feels what you feel,
When you're sad it rains,
When you're happy it's sunny,
When you're angry there's thunder and lightning,
Which can seem very frightening,
My role model is based on the leaves,
How they flow gently in the breeze.

Ponal Qureshi (12)
King Edward VI Handsworth School For Girls, Birmingham

My Hero: Jordan Clark

Jordan Clark is my hero
I say it all the time
I would talk about her perfect ginger hair
But 'ginger' is hard to rhyme.

She is on a TV show
It is called 'The Next Step'
And recently I saw her live
Dancing on a stage at the REP.

Her signature move is called The Spider
Where she twists her body around
Her feet walk around her head
While she lies calmly on the ground.

I met her twice when I had
A VIP pass backstage
And even better, an hour later
I saw her dance live on stage.

Jordan Clark is my hero
Always is, always will be
And I'm excited to see her next time
When she comes back to Birmingham City.

Kate Holmes (12)
King Edward VI Handsworth School For Girls, Birmingham

She'll Always Be My Hero

She'll always be my hero,
She makes me laugh every day,
She is perfect in every possible way,
She'll always be my hero,
Her products and her videos are almost as good as her looks,
One reason I love her is because she writes books,
She'll always be my hero,
Flawless and perfect, are what she is,
I could tell you some more in a whizz,
She'll always be my hero,
Her eyebrows are always on fleek,
Her clothes are pretty chic,
She'll always be my hero,
Creating hand sanitisers and mugs,
Did I mention that she's got a pug?
She'll always be my hero,
Most of all she always does her best,
It's as if she has no rest,
She'll always be my hero.

Arfah Khan (12)
King Edward VI Handsworth School For Girls, Birmingham

My Mum

My mum is always there,
Whether it is an exam,
Or a bruise.
My mum is my moral support.

My mum is always protecting me,
Like a shepherd looking after his sheep,
From harm.
My mum is my shield of love.

My mum is always forgiving my endless sins,
No matter how big or small,
But there to lead me away from evil.
My mum is my guide.

My mum is always waiting,
For me to come home from school,
Enveloping me in homely hugs and kisses.
My mum is comfort.

My mum is always sympathetic.
He good-natured words,
Avert me from temptation.
She is my valiant knight rescuing the damsel in distress.
My mum is my hero.

Chenyao Zhou (12)
King Edward VI Handsworth School For Girls, Birmingham

My Hero

My hero is someone

Who tucks me in when I am down
Who cheers me up when I've got a frown
Who takes care of my needs
Who makes sure I do good deeds
Who gives me a loving hug
Who saves me from little bugs
Who comforts me when I am scared
Who makes sure that I share
Who makes sure I am safe
Who always brings me a Jaffa Cake
Who does everything from cooking to cleaning
Who deserves her life story in a movie screening
Who puts others before herself
Who always worries about someone else
Many don't realise how much she does,
She really does deserve all the buzz

I know you may think it's dumb,
But my amazing hero is my mum!

Gurleen Klair (12)
King Edward VI Handsworth School For Girls, Birmingham

My Role Models

My mother, she is caring and sweet
She likes things to be tidy and neat
She is beautiful both on the inside and outside
She believes in modesty yet pride

My father is funny, witty but also strict
He always understands me
He has a solution to every conflict
He's practical, positive and just seems perfect

I love the way my grandma is
So simple yet so complicated
She is giving, caring, compassionate, kind and understanding
She knows me inside out like no one else can
She is special and unique to me.

My family always makes me smile!
Happiness that could stretch a thousand miles!
I love my family!
I hope to be like them!

Shriya Kashyap (12)
King Edward VI Handsworth School For Girls, Birmingham

The Idols Within Me!

My inspiration?
Or is it just my imagination?
A person in disguise,
Or are we all these just lies,
Truths unfold,
Whilst tales to be told,
Ways to help me in hard times,
Ways of stopping me from committing crimes,
Someone who will always be there!
Someone who gives me the ability to help and share!
To notice the world around me!
To make me mindful and aware;
Oh and yes, it's my humanity!
Now listen in and listen well!
As I have something to tell!
Whether you're big or small,
Whenever you're in the situation where you fall!
Pick yourself up!
There will always be a way!
If you believe in yourself,
That's all I can say!

Ayesha Sarfraz (12)
King Edward VI Handsworth School For Girls, Birmingham

My Furry Friend

He is always there for me
no matter where I go.
He is always there for me
with his fluffy, ginger coat.

He is loving and caring
even when we're ill.
He is loving and caring
when we're feeling down.

He is super relaxed
and sits on my lap.
He is super relaxed
and snores on his back.

He is super chilled
and lets me dress him up.
He is super chilled
and lets me pick him up.

He is my dog
I am his owner.
He is my dog
and he's called Fudge.

Fudge is my role model
even thought he's just a dog.
Fudge is my role model
like a gift from God.

Emily Warmington (12)
King Edward VI Handsworth School For Girls, Birmingham

Who Is My Role Model?

My role model is as caring as can be,
Under all her talents you may see.
My role model matters most to me,
She makes me happy like a buzzing bee.

She cannot fly,
Or soar the sky.
But love and care,
And hug better than a teddy bear.

She may not be a billionaire,
And have a butler everywhere.
But she loves me to bits,
Even when I get in fits.

I love her to the stars,
I would travel to Mars.
I would do anything for her,
Because she is my mother.

My role model is my mummy,
Unique, beautiful and funny.
My role model is my mum,
She smiles brighter than the gleaming sun.

Gurmeena Kaur Nahal (13)
King Edward VI Handsworth School For Girls, Birmingham

Shawn Mendes

Many people ask me who I look up to
Instead I look down and think about him
Shawn Mendes
I look up and stutter
Shawn Mendes.

They all snigger at me
As I think where would I be without him?
They all say
'How can you like him?
He's just a kid!'

And I reply with
No actually he's eighteen and a legal adult
And did you mean 'Kid in Love', his song?
'It's available on iTunes
You should totally buy it, you'd love it!'
I say as I snap my fingers and walk away.
Away from the petty haters.

I plug in my earphones
And hum Mercy.

Abigail Balfour (12)
King Edward VI Handsworth School For Girls, Birmingham

And I Love That...

You're as nutty as a squirrel,
You're as bright as the sun,
You're perfectly imperfect,
And I love that.

You always get your way,
You're not the best of cooks,
You feed me way too much,
And I love that.

You have that kind of face,
That's always soft and trusting,
You surround yourself with family,
And I love that.

Your house always smells of dog,
And birds and hamsters too,
You're crazy and play drums,
And I love that.

So every single day,
I strive to be like you,
I miss you to the moon and back,
And I love you!

Nancy Alice Rutter (13)
King Edward VI Handsworth School For Girls, Birmingham

My Heroes Wrapped In Newspaper

Although you may not think it's true,
I find my heroes as popular as a Gordon Ramsay stew.
They are a crisp autumn wood on the outside,
And soft and warm on the inside.
They are the best at any given time,
But some think they are a crime.

You might think they go with mayonnaise,
Chilli sauce puts them in a daze,
They are the best with tomato sauce.
I would have it for my first, second and third course.

You can find them at the local takeaway,
But in my house they are here to stay.
You can now begin to lick your lips,
Yes, they are chips.

Hana Amin (12)
King Edward VI Handsworth School For Girls, Birmingham

My Role Model

When I'm older,
And a little bit bolder,
I want to be,
A stronger version of me.
To help with this,
So I don't go amiss,
I look up to,
Somebody who,
Has style in her walks,
And does some great talks!
She is a famous actor,
And definitely has a wow factor,
That makes everyone stare,
Because she has that natural flare.
She is a passionate feminist,
All to her own benefit,
And her beliefs are strong,
But never wrong!
My role model is amazing,
Worthy of praising,
The one and only one
Emma Watson.

Nizara Ziaudeen (12)
King Edward VI Handsworth School For Girls, Birmingham

My Inspiration!

My role model does many things,
My role model is an inspiration,
People look up to celebrities,
I don't!

My role model writes many books,
My role model has many fans,
My role model is an author.

I have never met her,
I have only read her books,
Her books are inspiring,
She is Jacqueline Wilson!

Her books are about real life,
Her books make you think,
Her books give you advice,
Her books inspire me to write.

She is my inspiration!

Iqra Rehman (12)
King Edward VI Handsworth School For Girls, Birmingham

Kevin Clifton - A Strictly Star

My hero flies, glides across the floor,
Making stunning shapes with his body,
Expressing love and passion through the art of dance,
A teacher, a loyal friend,
Reaching out and helping others,
While making those around him smile.

From the jive to the tango,
He teaches friends to express emotion,
Through the movement and fluidity of the body,
I aspire to be like him,
Uplifting the sad,
And comforting and turning dark paths light.

You inspire me to have a dream.

Isabella Hickman (13)
King Edward VI Handsworth School For Girls, Birmingham

Saina Nerwal

Saina,
Saina,
Saina,
India's aspiration,
Turned into India's disappointment.

A somnolent, sleepy creature,
Yet fierce and full of raging anger,
Once a fragile butterfly,
Next she changed,
Into a potent tiger she grew.

She was extremely talented and notorious,
I was not,
Courageous and determination she showed,
I did not,
However I will.

She is a fantasy,
A need,
A want,
A desire,
My everything.

Dhairya Ruparelia (12)
King Edward VI Handsworth School For Girls, Birmingham

My Dad

He is the best of them all,
At least to me he is,
He knows everything from wives to flowcharts,
Flowcharts to metaphors,
Metaphors to bearings,
He knows it all.

Sharing the same love for everyone,
I enjoy every moment with him,
He taught me all,
And I shall know for evermore!
Blazing like the luminous sun above,
Shine eternal Blaze!

Audrey Ntelah (12)
King Edward VI Handsworth School For Girls, Birmingham

My Sweet Hero

My hero is always with me,
It is always by my side.
My hero I will always see,
And without it I will lose my mind.

My hero is my treat,
It gives me life.
My hero is a sweet,
And without it I will die.

Ramisa Mumith (12)
King Edward VI Handsworth School For Girls, Birmingham

Heather

Wonderful, clever, unique and downright fantastic are just a few
Of many words that describe the most marvellous person to
Walk the earth: my best friend. It would be cliché to say she's funny,
Cliché to say she's brilliant. But she is brilliant and she is helpful.
No one wipes tears better than her. There are many words to
describe how much I love her.
A most wonderful friendship knitted jumpers, baked biscuits.
Sassy comments would come first to mind when I think about her.
I am so thankful for such a wonderful, amazing and simply
fantastic best friend.
Thanks Heather.

Rhiannon Flynn (13)
Sanquhar Academy, Sanquhar

My Mum

There's no one like my mum.
She smiles at me when she's happy.
She hugs me when I'm upset
She cares for me when I'm hurt
There's nothing like my mum.

My mum is kind and happy
She's the best mum ever
She keeps on loving me
She's a great example of a mum.

My mum keeps a roof over my head
She cooks and cleans a lot
I do some work around the house
She buys me some things to make me happy
There is no one like my mum.

Keira Cunningham (12)
Sanquhar Academy, Sanquhar

All Time Low

A ll Time Low
L ove all their fans
E verywhere on Earth
'X tremly talented

G ives his
A ll no matter what
S how. Everywhere visited is always
K iller
A nd always makes it
R eal.
T he fact that he exists makes my
H eart fill with happiness.

Kerri Louise Freeburn (14)
Sanquhar Academy, Sanquhar

My Poetry Idol

Z oella is a YouTuber.
O pen-hearted and sweet.
E legant and good taste in style.
L ove her pug, Nala.
L ove her family and friends.
A lfie is Zoe's boyfriend.

Hannah Kenyon (13)
Sanquhar Academy, Sanquhar

Young Writers Information

We hope you have enjoyed reading this book – and that you will continue to in the coming years.

If you're a young writer who enjoys reading and creative writing, or the parent of an enthusiastic poet or story writer, do visit our website **www.youngwriters.co.uk**. Here you will find free competitions, workshops and games, as well as recommended reads, a poetry glossary and our blog.

If you would like to order further copies of this book, or any of our other titles, then please give us a call or visit **www.youngwriters.co.uk**.

Young Writers
Remus House
Coltsfoot Drive
Peterborough
PE2 9BF
(01733) 890066 / 898110
info@youngwriters.co.uk